This book belongs to

....

Designed by Nicola Butler
Edited by Lesley Sims
Fairies illustrated by Molly Sage and Nicola Butler
With thanks to Sara Matthews, Assistant Director at the Central School of Ballet
Additional story by Emma Helbrough
Photographic manipulation: John Russell

www.usborne.com
First published in 2004 by Usborne Publishing Ltd.,
Usborne House, 83-85 Saffron Hill, London ECIN 8RT, England. Copyright © 2004 Usborne Publishing Ltd.

The Usborne
Ballet Treasury

Susanna Davidson and Katie Daynes

Illustrated by
Shelagh McNicholas
and Nilesh Mistry

Contents

Being a
ballet dancer

Beginning ballet

Ballet makes you feel as light as a feather and as graceful as a bird. It also makes your body strong and supple. Dancers can leap, dart, spin and twirl with amazing grace and speed. Learning ballet is fun, exciting – even magical.

Ballet has been around for almost four hundred years.

Girls usually wear stretchy leotards over pink or white tights, and soft, pink shoes, while boys dress in t-shirts, shorts, socks and black shoes. Girls can add a wrap-around cardigan if they're cold. Long hair should be tied back with ribbons or in a tight, neat bun, so it doesn't get in your eyes.

Dance studios have lots of space for running around. Along the side, there are large mirrors so dancers can check their position as they move.

A wooden rail, called the *barre*, is attached to the wall. This helps dancers to balance while they work on their ballet exercises. There is often a piano in the corner and a pianist who plays during lessons, so everyone can learn to move to music.

Some ballet schools have a special wooden floor which springs a little when dancers jump. This is so they don't hurt their feet after leaping and spinning high up in the air.

Warming up

Ballet teachers start their lessons with gentle warm-up exercises, to make the dancers' muscles warm and stretchy. Lessons often begin with everyone sitting in a circle with their legs out in front of them. One of the easiest exercises is called Good toes, Naughty toes.

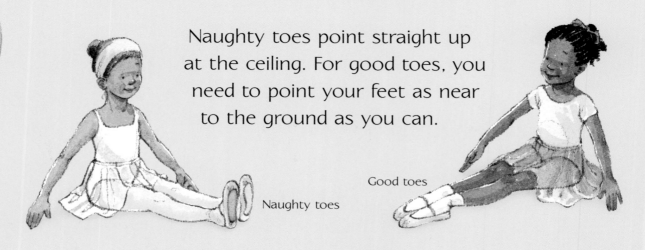

Naughty toes point straight up at the ceiling. For good toes, you need to point your feet as near to the ground as you can.

Good toes

Naughty toes

With everyone's feet warmed up, it's time to exercise the rest of the body. Gently reach your arms out in front of you, as if you're pushing away fluffy, white clouds.

Your legs must be flat on the ground. Pretend you've stuck them down with glue.

All ballet
movements are
soft and gentle.

Now imagine you have a basket by your side, full
of shining stars. Pick up each star between your thumb
and middle finger, then raise your arm to hang the
stars one by one across the night sky.

There are also exercises
you can do to stretch your body.
Try walking your hands down your legs,
as if your fingers are spiders' legs. Keep
going until you reach your feet. This bends
you gently forward.

When you stand, pull up your body so it's
tall and straight. It helps to hold in your tummy
and look straight ahead – as if you're wearing
a crown. Keep your back as flat as you can.
Only bad dancers look like bananas.

Try putting the arm
and leg positions together
in different ways.

Ballet steps

Say "ara-besk"

"Paa-duh-shaa"

"Pi-roo-et"

Ballet dancers know hundreds
of different steps. Many of them have
wonderful sounding names, like *arabesque*,
pas de chat and *pirouette*. But all dancers begin by
learning the five main positions.

First position

Second position

Third position

Fourth position

Fifth position

Ballet dancers put these positions together with spins
and whirls in the air. To stop them from getting dizzy,
they use a special trick called the spotting trick.

Try this trick slowly at first. Look at a spot straight
ahead, such as a mark on a wall, and keep looking at it
while you slowly turn around. At the last moment, whip
your head around and bring it back to focus on your spot.

Dancing on pointe
makes a dancer's
legs look longer.

If you go to a ballet, you'll see all the female dancers do steps on the very tips of their toes. This is called dancing on *pointe*. They make it look easy, but it takes years of training.

Female ballet dancers wear shoes, called pointe shoes, which are stiffened with glue at the end to help them balance. Pointe shoes have a layer of shiny satin on the outside and canvas on the inside. The shoes are tied on with pink satin ribbons.

Tuck in the loose ends of the ribbon. Ends that stick out are called pig's ears.

To tie ballet shoes, cross over the ribbons in front of your ankle. Take them around behind the ankle and cross them over again. Bring the ribbons back to the front and cross them over a last time. Then bring the ends around to the inside of your ankle and knot them securely.

Telling a story

Ballet is a way of telling a story without words, so dancers have to be able to act as well as dance. They use their bodies to show thoughts and feelings. Signs, called mimes, also help to tell the story. Some mimes are easy to understand. Others are more tricky.

Afraid

Please

Sleeping

Kill

Ballet dancers play many different characters. They can creep around like spies or prowl like lions. Sometimes they move their arms to make them look like wings or beaks. As witches, dancers hunch their shoulders and curl their fingers into claws.

This boy is being a bird.

Which one do
you think is the
wicked one?

Dancers wear amazing
costumes too. These often
show the audience if a
character is good or wicked.

Some ballet classes put on shows of their own, so
pupils have a chance to perform in front of an audience.
Everyone gets to dress up and paint their faces, and girls
might wear a tutu – a special ballet skirt made from
layers of stiff netting. Pupils may be nervous before
the show, but as soon as the music begins, they
can forget where they are and dance!

Ballet school

There are schools where ballet is just as important as English or science. Many pupils live there, and spend each day rushing between ballet and normal lessons. Somehow, they squeeze in music, drama, jazz and modern dance too.

8:45-10:15	Ballet class
10:30-11:30	Pointe work for girls Jumps for boys
12:00-1:00	Music
2:00-3:15	Pas de deux
3:30-5:30	School work

You can start full-time ballet school when you're eleven, but getting in is tough. Teachers watch everyone closely to see who has the shape and talent to become a professional dancer. Ballet dancers need long, graceful limbs, arched feet and a strong, supple back.

This powder will stop me slipping on the wooden floors.

As well as classrooms, ballet schools have huge studios with wooden floors. So students don't slip, they rub the soles of their shoes in white powder called rosin before they rehearse. Sometimes the younger students come to see the older ones at work. They watch in awe as the dancers fly through the air.

The last two years of ballet school are make or break time. Some students leave to become jazz dancers or ballet teachers. Others end up doing something completely different, like painting or poodle training.

Only the most determined and talented pupils become professional dancers. Ballet companies take on just a few dancers each year. They start off in the *corps de ballet*, performing as part of a group. Female dancers are known as ballerinas. Competition is fierce, but the ones who make it have an incredible life ahead of them.

Say "cor duh ballay"

17

A ballet dancer's day

Ballet dancers travel all over the world with different ballet companies, performing to thousands of people. But even the top stars still take classes every day.

Even *I* still have lessons, and I'm the Ballet Fairy.

Dancers begin with exercises at the *barre*, to work on their technique. Then they move to the middle of the studio, where they perform slow, complicated steps that get faster and faster. The lesson often ends with huge leaps, called *grands jetés*.

Say "gron jetay"

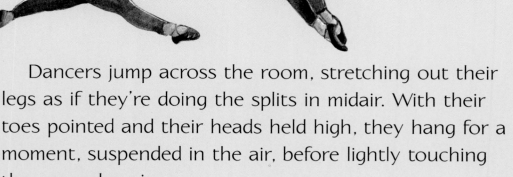

Dancers jump across the room, stretching out their legs as if they're doing the splits in midair. With their toes pointed and their heads held high, they hang for a moment, suspended in the air, before lightly touching the ground again.

The rest of the dancer's day is packed with rehearsals, often for as many as three or four different ballets. Dancers learn to switch quickly from one character to another. A dancer might be a good fairy in the morning and a wicked witch by the afternoon.

Partners rehearse together for a *pas de deux*, where a man and a woman dance in a pair. Male dancers must have strong muscles for lifting the ballerina, while the ballerina needs balance and strength to look like she's gliding effortlessly through the air.

Most evenings, it's showtime. Performing in front of an amazed audience makes all the hard work worthwhile. Only then, at the end of an action-packed day, can the dancers finally head home – usually for a long, hot and relaxing bath, to soothe their tired muscles.

Putting
on a show

Rehearsing

Two months before a show, ballet companies are humming with excitement. The ballet story has been chosen and the music has been written. A person called a choreographer has spent weeks coming up with dance ideas and now it's time for the first rehearsal.

Dancers don't just copy the choreographer, they suggest their own steps too. All day they dart, leap and glide until, finally, the choreographer is happy. The moves are recorded on video so no one forgets them, then everyone goes home. In the morning, rehearsals will start all over again.

Ballet dance steps are often written down as squiggles.

At first, dancers rehearse to piano music while the other musicians learn their parts. Snatches of melodies float down the corridor, followed by the conductor's stern voice. It's the conductor's job to train the orchestra and lead them during the show. If the music is too fast or too slow, the dancers on stage will be in trouble.

Meanwhile, a designer is busy thinking about the stage. When the curtains open, what will the audience see? Once the designer has dreamed up the scenes, a team of artists work hard to create them. Backgrounds are painted onto huge pieces of cloth. Chairs, tables and other props are lined up and lights are positioned to make the most of the stage.

With only a few days to go, everyone comes together for the final rehearsals. It's a nail-biting time. Any problems need to be ironed out quickly because people have already bought their tickets.

Costumes

No one will recognize me with this mask.

Each ballet company has a fantastic costume department made up of artists, tailors and wardrobe assistants. They make sure every dancer has a costume that fits and that it's ready in time for the final rehearsals.

A costume can start off as a scribble on a page. Artists draw up their ideas for each character and suggest wonderful fabrics. The tutu is the classic ballet outfit, but modern ballets are a good excuse for adventurous new costumes. As long as dancers can still move easily, anything goes.

To look the part, dancers need a face to match their costume. They also want the back row of the audience to see their features clearly. Eyeliner, eyeshadow, lipstick and rouge are all used in vast quantities, and that's only for the *corps de ballet*.

Main characters often need special face paints – warts for ugly sisters or beauty spots for princesses. Make-up artists can change a dancer's whole expression by adding slanty eyebrows or extra lipliner.

It's important to keep warm before going on stage.

On opening night, the cast gathers backstage. First they do their faces and hair, sitting in front of well-lit mirrors. Then they do warm-up exercises at the *barre*. Shortly before the show, they put on their costumes.

The show

With the stage ready and the curtains closed, the manager gives a sign for the main doors to open. The audience shuffles in with a rustle of coats, lots of chatter and muffled coughs. As they fill the seats, they hear the musicians tuning their instruments. If they crane their necks, they can see the orchestra, sunk down in a pit in front of the stage.

The best seats are usually in the middle, near the front.

Backstage, there's a call for "beginners" and the first dancers get into position. Slowly, the lights go down and the audience falls silent. Everyone waits for the conductor to enter and take a bow. With a wave of the baton, the music begins. Suddenly, the stage lights come on and the curtains float apart. Act One is about to begin...

Other dancers wait nervously in the dressing room. They listen to the music on small speakers, so they know exactly what's happening on stage. A minute before their scene, they gather silently in the wings.

Appearing on stage is an amazing experience. The stage lights are so dazzling, they block out the audience. Music soars up from the orchestra pit and the dancers become transformed into their characters. While they're on stage, nothing matters except the mesmerizing moves they know by heart.

Over the next couple of hours, the ballet story unfolds. Often there's an interval in the middle for drinks and ice cream. When the lights go down on the final scene, all that's left is the curtain call. A delighted audience loves to congratulate the dancers as they come forward to curtsey or bow.

Famous ballet stars

Darcey Bussell and Jonathan Cope dance a *pas de deux*.
Both tall and graceful, they are well matched.

Ballet stars scrapbook

Tiptoe Taglioni

Marie Taglioni was one of the world's first famous ballerinas. Born two hundred years ago, she was taught to dance by her father. In those days, ballet shoes weren't stiffened with glue, so dancing on *pointe* was very difficult. Marie rehearsed for six hours a day, until she could balance perfectly. When she starred in her father's ballet, *La Sylphide*, the audience went wild.

This is one of the shoes Marie Taglioni actually wore.

Rags to riches

In 1881, Anna Pavlova was born into a poor Russian family. She was a skinny child, and often unwell. When Anna was eight, her mother took her to see *The Sleeping Beauty*. By the interval, Anna knew she wanted to be a ballerina. At first, her teachers thought she was too weak and frail to dance, but she astonished them with her natural grace and talent.

30

The dying swan

Anna toured the world, delighting audiences everywhere. Her most famous dance was called *The Dying Swan*. Just before she died, she called out, "Prepare my swan costume."

Daring dancing

Vaslav Nijinsky was at ballet school with Anna Pavlova. His parents were dancers and he'd been performing since the age of three. The other students teased him for being small and having a Polish accent, but his dancing spoke for itself – it was so full of energy and ideas. Vaslav went on to choreograph and star in his own exciting ballets. At first, audiences were surprised by his new moves, but soon everyone wanted to see him perform.

31

The English snowflake

In the 1930s, a young English ballerina rose to fame. Her real name was Peggy Hookham, but on stage she was known as Margot Fonteyn. She made her first professional appearance as a snowflake, aged fifteen. The following year, the ballet company's top ballerina left and Margot took her place.

"Great artists are people who find the way to be themselves in their art."

Margot Fonteyn

Ashton at the ball

The choreographer and dancer, Frederick Ashton, was quick to notice Margot's talent. He created many roles to suit her flowing style and they worked together for the next twenty-five years. When choreographing *Cinderella*, he cast Margot as Cinders and himself as an ugly sister.

Frederick Ashton is the sister on the left with the big pearl necklace.

Forever young

After Margot Fonteyn's fortieth birthday, most of her fans thought she would retire, but then Rudolf Nureyev appeared. Together they starred in the ballet *Giselle* and – although Rudolf was almost twenty years younger – they made a perfect pair. Margot continued performing for the next ten years.

On the run

Rudolf Nureyev was born in Russia, on a train. By the age of twenty, he was a national ballet star. Since at that time most Russian citizens weren't allowed to leave their country, Rudolf was accompanied on world tours by Russian guards. While in France in 1961, he managed to escape his guards and flee to England. From then on, he was free to perform anywhere and he became an international legend.

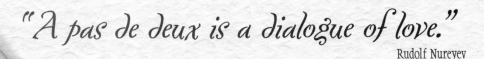

"A pas de deux is a dialogue of love."

Rudolf Nureyev

Tall and graceful

Darcey Bussell has been a leading ballerina for over fifteen years. She studied at the Royal Ballet School in London and took on her first major role aged nineteen. With her long legs and beautiful looks, she has worked as a model too.

Darcey is very tall for a ballerina, so her dance partners have to be chosen carefully.

Safe hands

Darcey's first dance partner, Jonathan Cope, has also enjoyed a long and successful career. Ballerinas love dancing with him because his strength and experience make them feel safe.

34

Cuban magic

Carlos Acosta, a Cuban dancer, almost never reached the stage. It was his dad, a truck driver, who sent him to ballet school. But Carlos used to skip classes to play soccer... until he saw the athletic Cuban ballet company perform and decided he wanted to join them.

"...no soccer player could be strong like that."
Carlos Acosta

Shooting stars

The dainty Romanian ballerina, Alina Cojocaru, shot from *corps de ballet* to principal dancer in only two years. Her pairing with Johan Kobborg has been a great success and together they've starred in *Swan Lake*, *The Nutcracker* and *Cinderella*.

A scene from The Nutcracker where Clara and the prince leave the snowy forest and head for the Land of Sweets.

Ballet stories

The Sleeping Beauty

Opening

Long ago, in a fairytale castle far away, a queen gave birth to a beautiful daughter and the king jumped for joy.

"Let's call her Aurora," suggested the queen.

"What a wonderful name," cried the king, "and let's invite all the fairies from our kingdom to her christening."

The day of the christening was sunny and bright. A graceful fairy dressed in lilac danced into the castle to greet the royal parents. Six more fairies followed, wearing vibrant summer dresses. One by one, they twirled up to Aurora in her cradle.

"I wish you beauty," said the first, waving her wand.

"A sweet temper," said the second,

"And grace," added the third.

"May you move like a ballerina," said the fourth.

"Sing like a nightingale," said the fifth.

"And play all the instruments of the orchestra perfectly," finished the sixth.

Before the Lilac fairy could add her gift, there was a crash of thunder and a black cloud blotted out the sun. From the darkness swept another fairy – the dreaded Carabosse – with her ugly rat servants prancing around her.

"Where was my invitation?" she spat, pointing a crooked finger at the king. "You have insulted me. Now I will give your daughter my gift." She turned her evil gaze on tiny Aurora. "I can't take away your beauty, my dear, but I can take away... your life. One day, something sharp will prick your finger and you will fall down DEAD!" As Carabosse's voice exploded into cackles, the other fairies cowered in a corner.

The poor queen couldn't hold back her tears. "Undo your curse," she pleaded. But Carabosse's cackling grew louder and louder, until the Lilac Fairy stepped forward and silenced her with a spell.

"Your Highness," said the Lilac Fairy, gently, "I still haven't offered your daughter my gift. Though I can't cancel Carabosse's curse, I can weaken it. Aurora will prick her finger and fall, but she won't die. She will slip into a deep sleep that can only be broken by the kiss of a handsome prince."

The fairy's kindness infuriated Carabosse. With a swirl of her cloak, she stormed from the castle. Slowly, the sun crept out from behind the cloud and spread light on the castle once more.

Act One

Princess Aurora grew prettier each day. The king and queen loved to watch their cheerful daughter dance and sing, but Carabosse's curse hung over them. All sharp objects were banished from the castle and the princess was never left alone.

For Aurora's sixteenth birthday, the king arranged a magnificent party. Sunshine flooded the royal gardens, guests met and mingled in the dappled shade and music floated on the warm summer air.

"Aurora," called the king, with a twinkle in his eye, "four birthday surprises have just arrived."

The princess laughed to see four nervous princes standing with her father. Tales of her beauty had reached distant kingdoms and now everyone wanted to marry her. The princes took turns dancing with Aurora. Charmed by her smile, each one offered his love and fortune. Aurora thanked them graciously, but she didn't want a husband – she just wanted to dance.

Twirling away from the fourth suitor, she spun into a wrinkled old lady. "Please excuse me," she said, sweetly.

"Don't worry, my dear," croaked the woman. "Look, I've brought you some flowers."

"How kind," said the princess, taking the bouquet.

Immediately, three worried courtiers swooped to grab the flowers. Aurora thought it was a game and danced away across the lawn, waving the flowers above her head. As she tightened her grip, she felt a sharp prick. "Ow!" she cried, dropping the bouquet and looking at her hand. A little drop of blood formed on her fingertip. Her dance turned into a sway and the world started spinning. Faces blurred and merged into one, then everything went blank.

The guests stared in horror as the princess fell to the ground. A familiar cackle filled the air and the old woman threw back her hood. It was Carabosse. After a gleeful look at the fallen princess, the evil fairy fled the castle grounds.

"My darling daughter!" cried the queen, rushing to Aurora's side. She lifted a lifeless arm and gasped.

A swirl of purple announced the Lilac Fairy. "Remember, she's not dead, only sleeping," the fairy said softly. "Take her into the castle and lie her on her bed."

Four courtiers carried the princess inside and the party guests followed in a hushed procession. Left alone in the garden, the Lilac Fairy watched as creepers and vines swiftly covered the castle walls. In no time, the building was overgrown and everyone inside was slumbering peacefully.

Act Two

One hundred years later, many miles from Aurora's palace, a royal hunt was taking place in a forest. While courtiers on horseback galloped after a deer, Prince Florimund and his guests stopped for a rest in a clearing.

"Let's dance!" suggested one of the pretty ladies. The men were all keen – except for Prince Florimund. He forced himself to smile and bow to his dance partner, but secretly he was bored.

"Another dance!" cried a lord.

"Not now," replied the prince. "You'd better catch up with the hunt before you lose them."

"Aren't you coming too?" said the lord.

"No, don't worry about me," he sighed. "I want to be alone."

The guests were surprised, but didn't like to argue. As they left the leafy glade, Florimund was already slumped in gloomy thoughts. But why did he feel so fed up? He was a prince – what more could he want in life? As Florimund sighed again, a fairy dressed in lilac appeared.

"You look sad," she said. "Let me show you something to lift your spirits." She swept her wand through the air and a vision of a princess flashed in front of the prince.

When Florimund blinked and looked again, there stood Princess Aurora, surrounded by fairies.

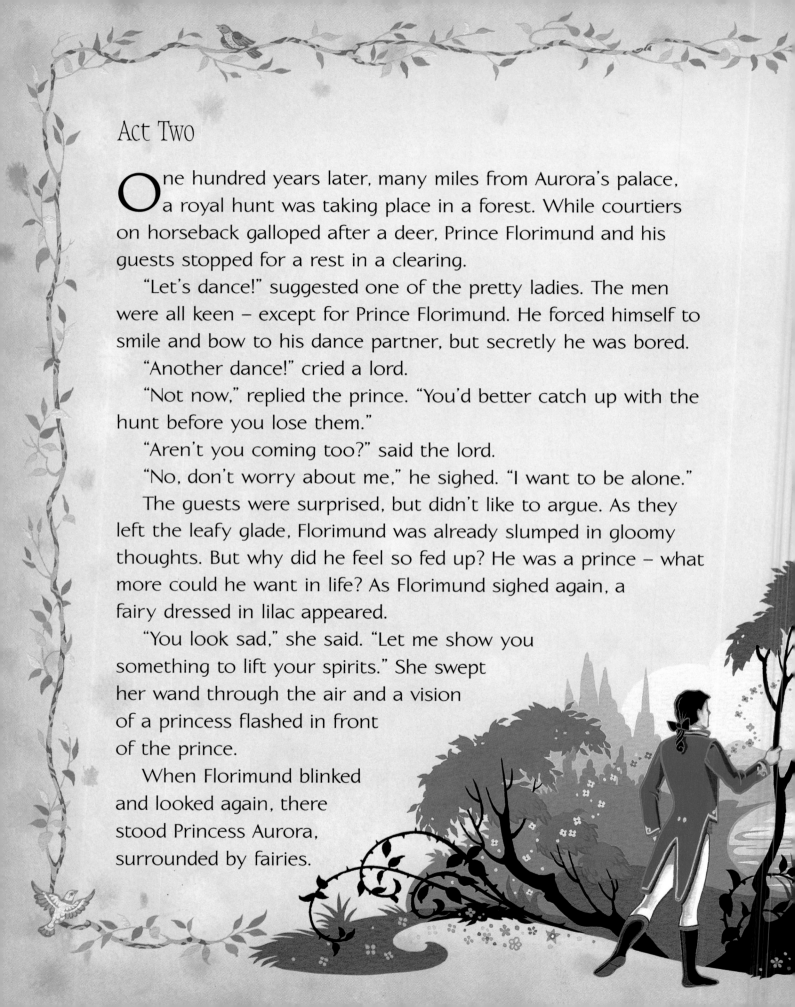

Her grace and beauty made him want to reach out and touch her. He took a step forward, but the fairies blocked his path. He tiptoed left, then right – his eyes never leaving the princess's face. Finally, he was close enough to embrace her, but in that instant she was gone.

The enchanted prince turned to the Lilac Fairy. "Who was that?" he asked. "Where has she gone? I've never seen anyone so wonderful in my life. I must find her!"

"Then follow me," said the fairy. From the glade, through the forest, the fairy guided Florimund. His step was quick but she was quicker, dancing over logs and streams. At last, they reached a shimmering lake and boarded a fairy boat. As they glided over silver water, the fairy pointed to a distant tower.

"The princess is sleeping in there," she said.

Florimund felt his heart beating faster. "Then I will go and wake her," he replied.

Act Three

The castle entrance was barely visible under a century of creepers and cobwebs. Prince Florimund strode up to the rusting gates and boldly pushed them apart. Fighting his way through the overgrown garden, he eventually reached the castle steps. When he creaked open the oak doors, he saw two footmen sprawled on the floor. Their deep breathing told him they were simply asleep. Then the Lilac Fairy was by his side, her shining wand casting light down the dark corridor.

"This way," she whispered.
She led the prince through the silent castle,
up a forgotten spiral staircase and into the princess's room.
Aurora lay on a four-poster bed, as pale as her silk pillow
and perfectly still.

"She's dead!" cried the prince.

"No, only sleeping," said the fairy, "and waiting for
you to wake her."

The prince had never spoken to the
princess and didn't even know her name. All he knew
was he wanted to kiss her. As their lips touched, Aurora's
eyes opened. Florimund stood back, embarrassed, but
Aurora held out her hand.

"Thank you," she whispered.

The delighted prince helped Aurora to her feet and led her
down the stairs. He was so dazzled by her beauty, he didn't see
the castle change around him. The creepers and vines melted
away and, all over the castle, people woke from their long sleep.

"Come and meet my parents," said Aurora to her prince.

She whisked him to the main hall, where her parents were
dusting their crowns.

"Aurora!" cried the king and queen.

"What a lovely name," thought the prince.

"Meet the prince who broke Carabosse's spell!" cried the
princess. She turned to smile at her rescuer, but he was kneeling
on the floor.

"Aurora," he said, "will you marry me?"

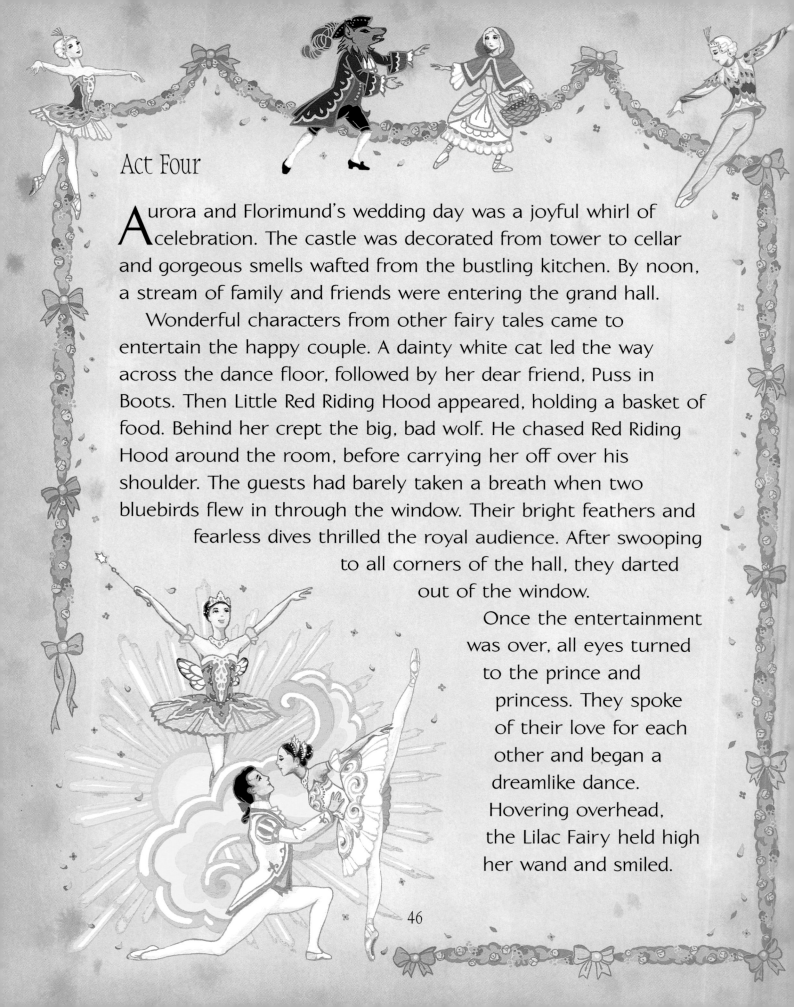

Act Four

Aurora and Florimund's wedding day was a joyful whirl of celebration. The castle was decorated from tower to cellar and gorgeous smells wafted from the bustling kitchen. By noon, a stream of family and friends were entering the grand hall.

Wonderful characters from other fairy tales came to entertain the happy couple. A dainty white cat led the way across the dance floor, followed by her dear friend, Puss in Boots. Then Little Red Riding Hood appeared, holding a basket of food. Behind her crept the big, bad wolf. He chased Red Riding Hood around the room, before carrying her off over his shoulder. The guests had barely taken a breath when two bluebirds flew in through the window. Their bright feathers and fearless dives thrilled the royal audience. After swooping to all corners of the hall, they darted out of the window.

Once the entertainment was over, all eyes turned to the prince and princess. They spoke of their love for each other and began a dreamlike dance. Hovering overhead, the Lilac Fairy held high her wand and smiled.

46

The Nutcracker

Act One

It was Christmas Eve and Dr. Stahlbaum was holding a party. One by one the guests arrived, shaking snow from their shoes before stepping into the warm, welcoming house. Soon everyone was laughing and talking, while the children danced and played in front of a magnificent Christmas tree.

The last guest to arrive was an old man in a heavy black cloak. His strange clothes and craggy face frightened some of the children. As he came into the room, they stopped dancing and rushed over to hide behind their parents.

The old man was Drosselmeyer, a good friend of Dr. Stahlbaum's and godfather to his two children, Clara and Fritz. "Don't be afraid, children," said Drosselmeyer, gently. "Just look what I have brought to show you."

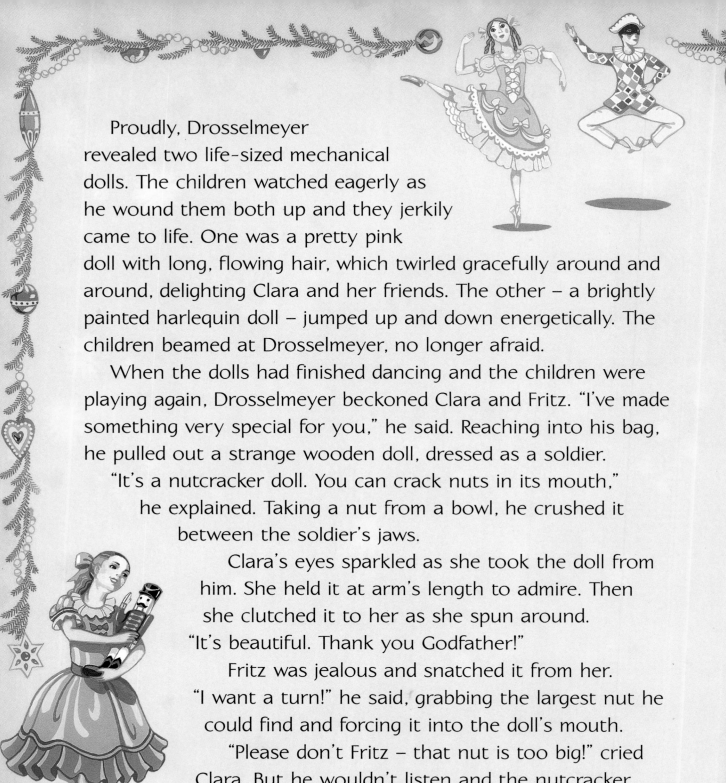

Proudly, Drosselmeyer revealed two life-sized mechanical dolls. The children watched eagerly as he wound them both up and they jerkily came to life. One was a pretty pink doll with long, flowing hair, which twirled gracefully around and around, delighting Clara and her friends. The other – a brightly painted harlequin doll – jumped up and down energetically. The children beamed at Drosselmeyer, no longer afraid.

When the dolls had finished dancing and the children were playing again, Drosselmeyer beckoned Clara and Fritz. "I've made something very special for you," he said. Reaching into his bag, he pulled out a strange wooden doll, dressed as a soldier.

"It's a nutcracker doll. You can crack nuts in its mouth," he explained. Taking a nut from a bowl, he crushed it between the soldier's jaws.

Clara's eyes sparkled as she took the doll from him. She held it at arm's length to admire. Then she clutched it to her as she spun around. "It's beautiful. Thank you Godfather!"

Fritz was jealous and snatched it from her. "I want a turn!" he said, grabbing the largest nut he could find and forcing it into the doll's mouth.

"Please don't Fritz – that nut is too big!" cried Clara. But he wouldn't listen and the nutcracker broke in half. Fritz dropped it and darted away. With tears in her eyes, Clara picked up the pieces and handed them to her godfather.

"Don't worry, my dear," he said, "I'll soon have this mended."

The evening sped by, and all too soon the party drew to an end. That night, Clara couldn't sleep. As the clock struck midnight, she crept downstairs to see if she could find the nutcracker doll. The room looked eerie in the dark and Clara trembled as she tiptoed around it. Her doll lay in front of the Christmas tree. As she bent down to pick it up, something incredible happened. The tree began to grow. It grew taller and taller until it brushed the ceiling. Then Clara heard a scratching sound behind her and spun around. Huge, mean-looking mice, each one as big as Fritz, were scampering out of the corners, swishing their tails and twitching their noses.

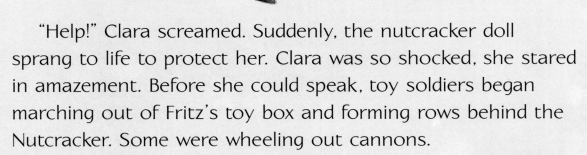

"Help!" Clara screamed. Suddenly, the nutcracker doll sprang to life to protect her. Clara was so shocked, she stared in amazement. Before she could speak, toy soldiers began marching out of Fritz's toy box and forming rows behind the Nutcracker. Some were wheeling out cannons.

"Prepare for battle!" cried the Nutcracker.

As the mice crept closer, the soldiers began to fire. Soon every mouse and soldier was locked in battle, slashing their swords to and fro. One by one, they fell wounded to the floor.

Then, out of the shadows sprang an even meaner mouse with a sneer on his face. He wore a crown and had a black patch over one eye.

"That's the Mouse King," whispered the Nutcracker, jumping firmly in front of Clara.

"Hand over the girl," bellowed the Mouse King.

"Never," the Nutcracker replied.

"Then you must die," jeered the Mouse King, thrusting his sword forward. The Nutcracker fought bravely, but he was neither quick enough nor strong enough to hold back the Mouse King. Soon he was backed into a corner. Clara thought fast. A few more seconds and her friend would be dead. She took off her shoe and hurled it as hard as she could at the Mouse King's head. He slumped to the ground, unconscious. Clara was so overcome with shock and relief that she fainted.

When Clara woke up, all the mice and soldiers had vanished. The Nutcracker stood before her, but he no longer resembled a strange-looking doll. He had been transformed into a handsome prince.

Clara smiled shyly.

"Thank you for saving my life," the prince said with a bow. "Please let me repay your bravery. Come with me to my homeland, as my special guest."

As he spoke, the walls of the house began to fade and a snowy forest grew up around them. The snow was so heavy that the trees looked as if they had been coated in thick, white icing.

The prince took Clara's hand as they weaved in and out of the trees, the snow crunching under their feet. "Don't worry, it's not far away," he promised. Clara looked up and saw huge snowflakes begin to fall from the night sky. As they neared the ground, the snowflakes changed into dancing ice fairies. She paused to watch their flitting movements, each perfectly in time with the others.

Act Two

When the pair reached the edge of the forest, Clara gazed in amazement at the sights before her. Wherever she turned, everything looked good enough to eat. The trees were giant lollipops, the rivers flowed with chocolate and the houses were made of gingerbread.

"Where are we?" Clara asked, in a stunned whisper.

"This is my homeland – the Land of Sweets," replied the prince, with a smile. Clara wanted to taste everything around her. "There's no time for that!" the prince insisted, dragging her away from a marshmallow toadstool. "I want to introduce you to someone very special indeed."

They hurried on over jellybean cobbles until they reached a pink palace made of sugar candy. As they began to climb the palace steps, a fanfare sounded and pink lemonade spouted dramatically from ornate fountains. At the top of the steps stood a beautiful lady wearing the prettiest lace dress Clara had ever seen, made of delicate spun sugar.

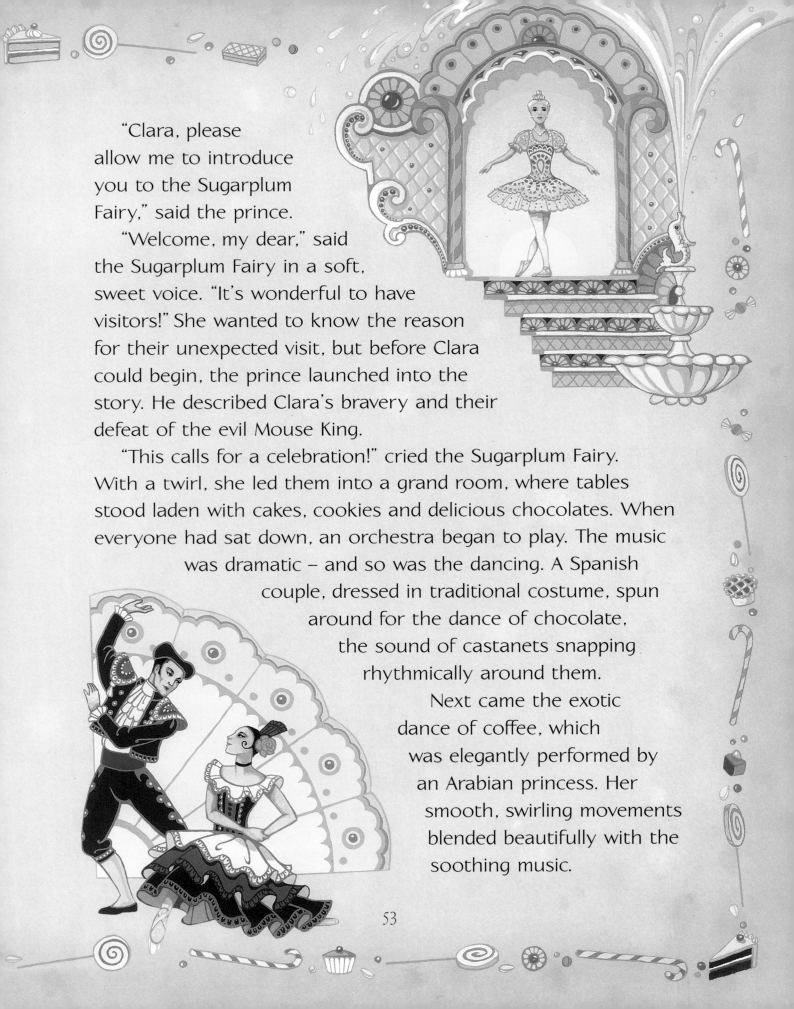

"Clara, please allow me to introduce you to the Sugarplum Fairy," said the prince.

"Welcome, my dear," said the Sugarplum Fairy in a soft, sweet voice. "It's wonderful to have visitors!" She wanted to know the reason for their unexpected visit, but before Clara could begin, the prince launched into the story. He described Clara's bravery and their defeat of the evil Mouse King.

"This calls for a celebration!" cried the Sugarplum Fairy. With a twirl, she led them into a grand room, where tables stood laden with cakes, cookies and delicious chocolates. When everyone had sat down, an orchestra began to play. The music was dramatic – and so was the dancing. A Spanish couple, dressed in traditional costume, spun around for the dance of chocolate, the sound of castanets snapping rhythmically around them.

Next came the exotic dance of coffee, which was elegantly performed by an Arabian princess. Her smooth, swirling movements blended beautifully with the soothing music.

53

The third dancer had come all the way from China to entertain everyone with his tea dance. He finished with a sweeping bow to Clara and the Sugarplum Fairy.

The evening continued with dance after dance. Each one represented something good to eat or drink with carefully chosen music and movements. Clara had never seen such a wonderful display. "I wish this evening would never end," she whispered in the prince's ear.

Finally came two very different dances. A group of ballerinas, each one dressed as a radiant flower, delicately performed a slow waltz for Clara. Their arms unfolded gracefully like the petals of a flower blooming. They weaved in and out of each other before finally finishing in a beautiful bouquet.

The very last dance of all was reserved for the Sugarplum Fairy and the prince. Their graceful steps almost moved Clara to tears.

As the final dance ended, Clara knew it would soon be time for her to return home. She rushed over and kissed the Sugarplum Fairy, thanking her over and over for making her feel so welcome in the Land of Sweets. "You will always be welcome here, my dear," the Sugarplum Fairy replied.

After thanking each and every dancer, Clara turned to the prince. "Is it time for us to say goodbye too?" she asked, quietly. The prince paused, before answering with a nod. Clara reached up and hugged him, shutting her eyes tightly.

When Clara opened her eyes again, she was no longer in the Land of Sweets. She was back in her own home, lying under the Christmas tree, with her nutcracker doll tucked under one arm. The first rays of morning sunlight were bouncing in through the window, melting the ice on the window ledge.

"It wasn't just a dream was it?" Clara murmured, shaking her nutcracker doll. But the doll simply stared back and said nothing.

Swan Lake

Act One

The castle was buzzing with excitement. It was Prince Siegfried's twenty-first birthday and the celebrations were just beginning. The royal servants rushed around putting the finishing touches to the feast. Some carried the last of the great jugs of wine to the tables outside, while others lit lanterns that hung from the trees. The assembled villagers gazed around in delight. A small girl tugged at her mother's hand. "It's like fairyland!" she said.

Their lively chatter was broken by a fanfare of trumpets, followed by the shout of a royal courtier. "Make way, make way," he cried, "Prince Siegfried is coming!" The prince strode out through the castle arch and the villagers raised their glasses to toast him. "Happy Birthday, Your Highness," they chorused.

Prince Siegfried smiled and waved in welcome. "Let the dancing begin!" he said.

The orchestra struck up a waltz and the courtyard was suddenly alive with movement. Couples twirled across the flagstones as the swell of violins filled the air.

Prince Siegfried looked on, laughing and joking with the villagers. Then he saw the anxious face of his friend beside him.

"What is it, Benno?" he asked.

"The Queen is coming," Benno whispered in reply.

As the villagers saw the Queen approach they grew silent.

The orchestra stopped playing and the dancers froze. The Queen made her way through the crowd, heading straight for her son. She held her head high and walked with purpose.

"Happy Birthday, my son," she said to Siegfried. Then she turned and beckoned to one of the servants. "Here is my present for you." Prince Siegfried gasped as he was handed a silver crossbow.

"Thank you, Mother," he began. "It's a wonderful present..." But the Queen raised her hand to silence him.

"Now you are twenty-one, it's time you behaved like a man. I have invited the most beautiful ladies in the kingdom to the ball tomorrow night – and I want you to marry one of them."

Prince Siegfried bowed politely. "As you wish," he said.

As soon as the Queen had gone, the music started again. The villagers laughed and danced around the tables. Prince Siegfried sat still, in the middle of it all, talking to no one.

"Cheer up," said Benno, laying a hand on his shoulder.

"I'm not ready to get married," said Siegfried, sighing heavily. "I'm too young."

"Well, you've still got tonight," said Benno. As he spoke, a flock of swans passed overhead, their bodies silhouetted against the evening sky.

"Let's go hunting!" Benno cried, pointing up at the swans. "You can try out your new crossbow. Come on!"

Siegfried watched the wild birds for a moment, listening for the sound of their powerful wing beats as they disappeared into the gathering darkness.

"Good idea!" Siegfried jumped to his feet and snatched up his crossbow. "Follow me!" he called to his friends, and they set out in pursuit of the swans.

Act Two

Siegfried and his friends tracked the swans through the royal forest, running down its twisting paths until they reached the shores of a lake.

"Go on ahead," Siegfried whispered to his friends. "I'll hide here." As his friends disappeared from sight, Siegfried crouched low behind a tree.

The water gleamed in the silvery moonlight. Siegfried watched and waited, his crossbow ready at his side. After a few moments, he spied the swans gliding silently across the lake's surface. With a steady hand he drew back his crossbow and took aim. But before he had time to release the arrow, the nearest swan rose out of the water. There was a flurry of beating wings and Siegfried gazed in wonder. In the place of the swan was a beautiful woman, stepping gracefully out of the water. She wore a downy white dress and on her head sat a feathered crown.

"Who are you?" Siegfried asked. The woman drew back in terror, but Siegfried quickly dropped his crossbow. "I won't hurt you," he said. The woman stood where she was, as if unsure. "I promise," Siegfried added.

"I am Odette," she said in a lilting voice, "Queen of the Swans."

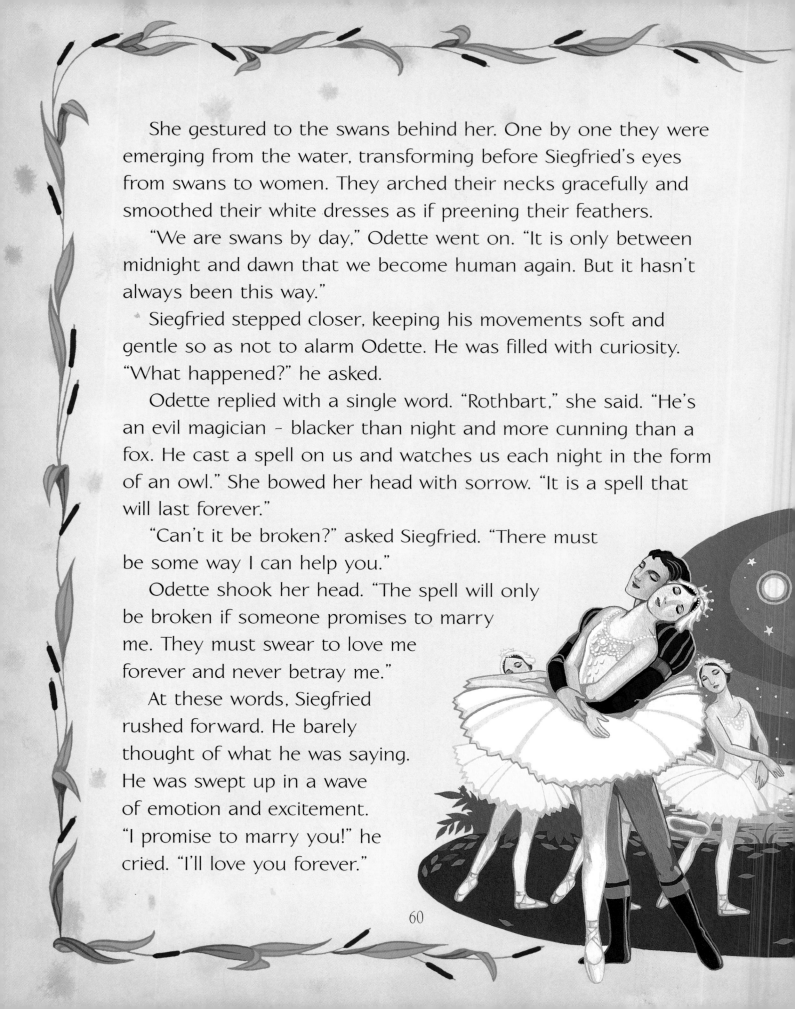

She gestured to the swans behind her. One by one they were emerging from the water, transforming before Siegfried's eyes from swans to women. They arched their necks gracefully and smoothed their white dresses as if preening their feathers.

"We are swans by day," Odette went on. "It is only between midnight and dawn that we become human again. But it hasn't always been this way."

Siegfried stepped closer, keeping his movements soft and gentle so as not to alarm Odette. He was filled with curiosity. "What happened?" he asked.

Odette replied with a single word. "Rothbart," she said. "He's an evil magician – blacker than night and more cunning than a fox. He cast a spell on us and watches us each night in the form of an owl." She bowed her head with sorrow. "It is a spell that will last forever."

"Can't it be broken?" asked Siegfried. "There must be some way I can help you."

Odette shook her head. "The spell will only be broken if someone promises to marry me. They must swear to love me forever and never betray me."

At these words, Siegfried rushed forward. He barely thought of what he was saying. He was swept up in a wave of emotion and excitement. "I promise to marry you!" he cried. "I'll love you forever."

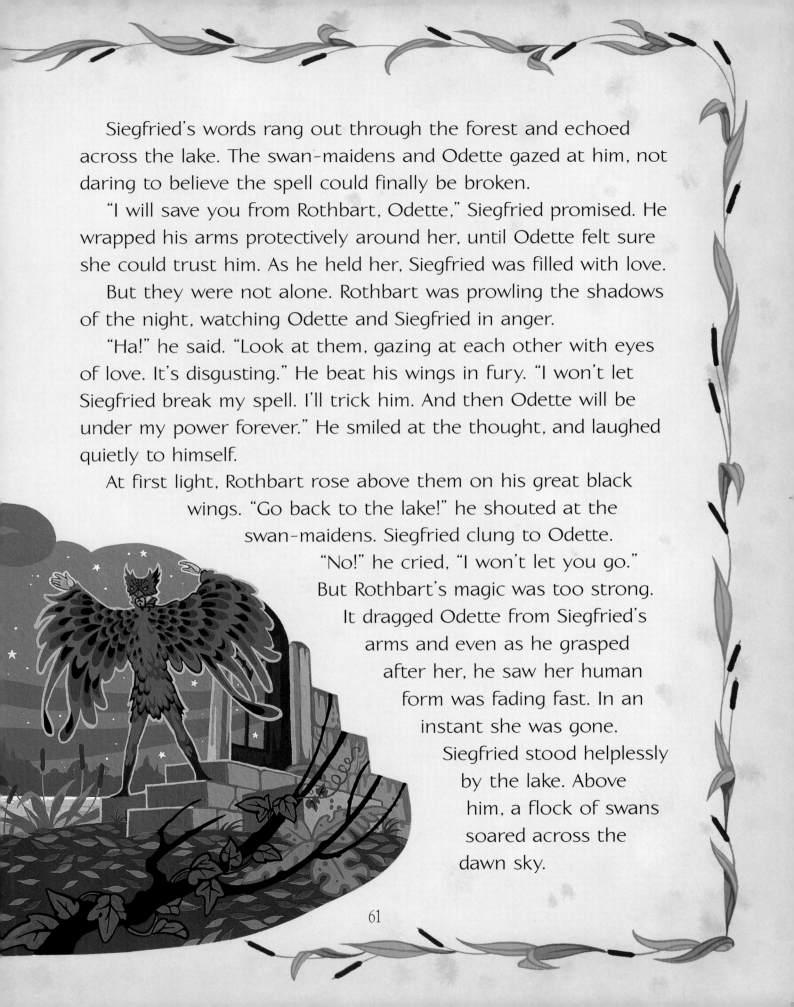

Siegfried's words rang out through the forest and echoed across the lake. The swan-maidens and Odette gazed at him, not daring to believe the spell could finally be broken.

"I will save you from Rothbart, Odette," Siegfried promised. He wrapped his arms protectively around her, until Odette felt sure she could trust him. As he held her, Siegfried was filled with love.

But they were not alone. Rothbart was prowling the shadows of the night, watching Odette and Siegfried in anger.

"Ha!" he said. "Look at them, gazing at each other with eyes of love. It's disgusting." He beat his wings in fury. "I won't let Siegfried break my spell. I'll trick him. And then Odette will be under my power forever." He smiled at the thought, and laughed quietly to himself.

At first light, Rothbart rose above them on his great black wings. "Go back to the lake!" he shouted at the swan-maidens. Siegfried clung to Odette.

"No!" he cried, "I won't let you go." But Rothbart's magic was too strong. It dragged Odette from Siegfried's arms and even as he grasped after her, he saw her human form was fading fast. In an instant she was gone.

Siegfried stood helplessly by the lake. Above him, a flock of swans soared across the dawn sky.

Act Three

It was the night of the birthday ball. The castle was crammed with guests and entertainers, who had journeyed from Spain, Hungary, Poland and Italy. The great hall glowed with fiery candles and the air was thick with perfume. The Queen sat on her purple throne and studied her son.

Siegfried was dutifully dancing with all the ladies she'd invited to the ball, but she had a feeling he didn't care for any of them. He barely looked at each one as they danced. Then he quickly led them back to their seats, before hurrying away. The Queen was furious.

"Siegfried must marry soon," she thought. "It's his duty as a prince." The Queen waited for the dancing to finish, then, as the last dance came to an end, she walked over to Siegfried.

"So, my son," she said, "which of these beautiful princesses are you going to take as your wife?" There was a hushed silence around the room and Siegfried's voice rang out clearly.

"I cannot marry any of them," he declared. He could think only of Odette.

The princesses blushed with embarrassment. The Queen looked furious, but before she could speak again there was a loud thunderclap and the door to the great hall was flung open. In the entrance stood two mysterious visitors. One was a tall man, dressed in the rich clothes of a Count.

He had thick black hair that rose up in almost feather-like tufts around his head, and there was something sinister about his dark, piercing eyes. But Siegfried only had eyes for the woman by his side. She too was dressed in black and on her head she wore a silver crown.

"Odette?" cried Siegfried, rushing to greet her. He was sure it was Odette. As the music began again, Siegfried invited the woman to dance. They whirled across the room and Siegfried felt himself bewitched by her beauty. He forgot about his mother, the other guests, the great hall... he could only stare into her glittering eyes. He never heard the sound of fluttering wings against the window. He never noticed the white shadow in the moonlight, gazing mournfully at Siegfried as he danced.

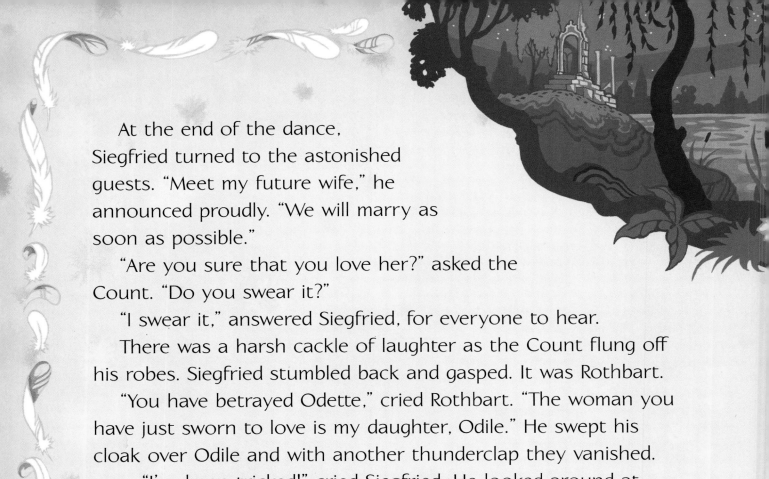

At the end of the dance,
Siegfried turned to the astonished
guests. "Meet my future wife," he
announced proudly. "We will marry as
soon as possible."

"Are you sure that you love her?" asked the
Count. "Do you swear it?"

"I swear it," answered Siegfried, for everyone to hear.

There was a harsh cackle of laughter as the Count flung off
his robes. Siegfried stumbled back and gasped. It was Rothbart.

"You have betrayed Odette," cried Rothbart. "The woman you
have just sworn to love is my daughter, Odile." He swept his
cloak over Odile and with another thunderclap they vanished.

"I've been tricked!" cried Siegfried. He looked around at
the shocked guests and tore from the room
without another word.

Act Four

Siegfried sped as fast as he could to the lake, his feet barely touching the ground. He found the swan-maidens huddled around Odette, trying to calm her. Siegfried threw himself at Odette's feet.

"Forgive me," he begged. "I was tricked by Rothbart but I never stopped loving you."

Odette looked up at Siegfried. Tears glistened on her cheeks. She had wept as she'd watched Siegfried dance with Odile, and wept again when she realized Rothbart's spell would never be broken. But hearing Siegfried's words she grew happy again.

"I felt something was wrong," she told him. "I came to the castle to warn you, but I couldn't get in. I watched you from the window and saw you dance with a woman dressed in black. You looked as if you loved her – but I felt sure she was evil."

"It was Odile, Rothbart's daughter," Siegfried explained. "He used his magic to make her look like you. Please forgive me Odette."

"I forgive you," Odette replied, and embraced him.

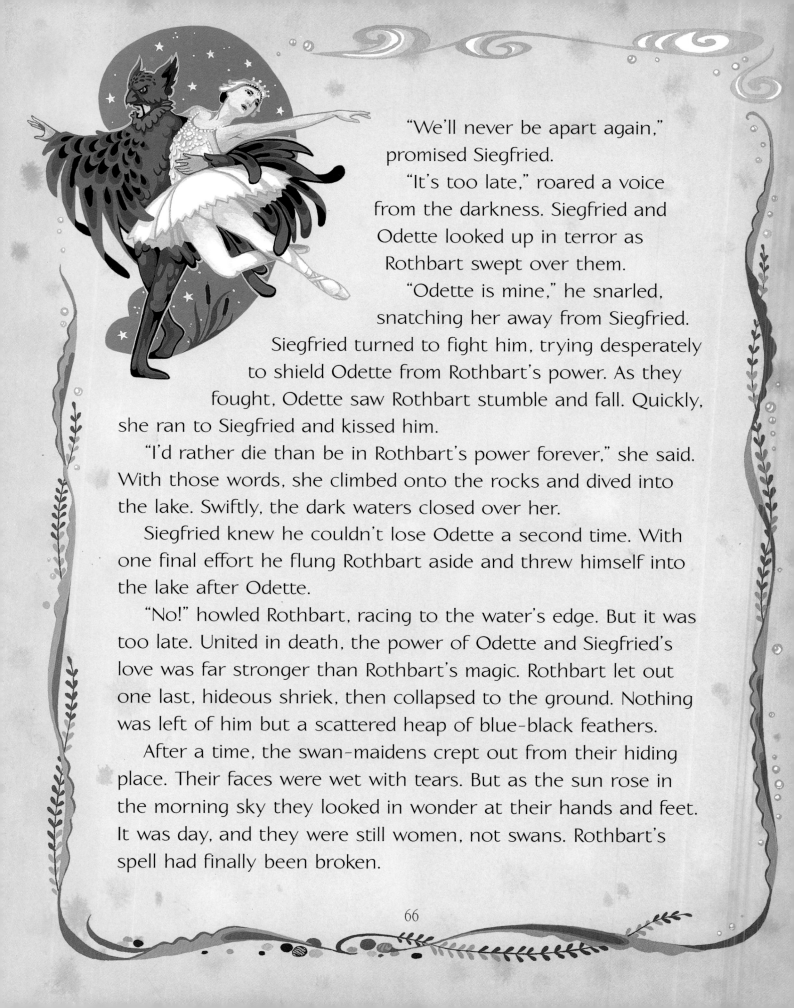

"We'll never be apart again," promised Siegfried.

"It's too late," roared a voice from the darkness. Siegfried and Odette looked up in terror as Rothbart swept over them.

"Odette is mine," he snarled, snatching her away from Siegfried.

Siegfried turned to fight him, trying desperately to shield Odette from Rothbart's power. As they fought, Odette saw Rothbart stumble and fall. Quickly, she ran to Siegfried and kissed him.

"I'd rather die than be in Rothbart's power forever," she said. With those words, she climbed onto the rocks and dived into the lake. Swiftly, the dark waters closed over her.

Siegfried knew he couldn't lose Odette a second time. With one final effort he flung Rothbart aside and threw himself into the lake after Odette.

"No!" howled Rothbart, racing to the water's edge. But it was too late. United in death, the power of Odette and Siegfried's love was far stronger than Rothbart's magic. Rothbart let out one last, hideous shriek, then collapsed to the ground. Nothing was left of him but a scattered heap of blue-black feathers.

After a time, the swan-maidens crept out from their hiding place. Their faces were wet with tears. But as the sun rose in the morning sky they looked in wonder at their hands and feet. It was day, and they were still women, not swans. Rothbart's spell had finally been broken.

The Firebird

Scene One

It was a glorious September day and Prince Ivan was out with his friends. They were exploring an overgrown forest when, somehow, he lost the others. "Wait for me!" he called, but no one heard. Ivan shrugged. With the sun warm on his back, he was happy to wander. In the distance wisps of bonfire smoke curled into the sky. Ivan could taste them in the air.

After a while, he came across a high stone wall and, curious to see what lay behind, quickly clambered to the top. Beneath him lay a magical garden, with rambling roses and statues entwined in ivy. In the very middle, he saw a tree, its spreading branches heavy with shining golden apples. Beyond the garden, protected by huge iron gates, stood a magnificent castle.

Ivan gasped. "This is surely an enchanted place," he thought, leaping from the wall onto the mossy grass below.

As he landed, there was a flash of brilliant yellow above him. Ivan glanced up. Swooping through the trees was a magnificent bird with feathers like flames.

"The Firebird?" Ivan wondered. He'd heard many stories about this magical creature, but he had never thought he'd actually see her. Ivan held his breath, standing completely still as the bird danced from branch to branch. "She's so beautiful," he thought, picturing her on display in a golden cage. Moving silently, he hid behind a statue and waited.

With a sweep of her glorious wings, the Firebird flew down onto a pile of leaves. Ivan sprang from his hiding place and caught her in his hands. The Firebird struggled, but Ivan held her tight. "Shh," he soothed. "I won't harm you. I just want to show you to my friends."

"No..." The Firebird shook her head despairingly.

"You'll be well cared for," Ivan promised. "You'll eat the finest food and live in a cage of gold."

"But that *will* harm me," the Firebird cried. "If you keep me locked up, I'll die!" Her dark eyes looked pleadingly at him. "If you have any pity in your soul, please, set me free."

Ivan looked at the splendid bird. He could feel her trembling in his hands. "I cannot keep you if it means your death," he sighed. "Go then, fly free." And throwing wide his arms he let the Firebird go.

To his surprise, she didn't soar away at once but stayed, hovering beside him. "Thank you prince," she said. "You didn't have to set me free. Now I shall repay your kindness." Bending her head, she tugged a feather from her chest and held it out to Ivan. Gently, he took it, admiring the way it glowed in the late afternoon sun.

The Firebird stretched her wings and rose into the air. "If you're ever in trouble," she called, "just wave the feather and I'll come."

"Thank you," Ivan began, but the Firebird had gone, her tail streaming behind her like a firework's trail. Ivan carefully put the feather in his pocket and turned to go, when he heard voices. Slipping behind the statue again, he watched a group of twelve girls creep through the gates that barred the way to the castle.

At first, their heads were bowed and their faces glum. But as they came deeper into the garden, their spirits seemed to lift. They were followed by the prettiest girl Ivan had ever seen. She seemed to glide among the statues like a princess. But though she smiled at her companions, her eyes were sad and she didn't say a word. Ivan's heart began to beat faster. Who was she?

Laughing and chattering, the other girls began to dance. Two of them plucked golden apples from the tree and began to play catch. They were so taken up with the game, they didn't notice Ivan come out from behind the statue. One of the apples flew in his direction and he jumped up to catch it. The girls stared at him, moving protectively around their silent companion. Ivan quickly bowed, offering the apple to the girl closest to him. But before he could speak, she bombarded him with questions. "Who are you? What are you doing here? Don't you know this garden belongs to the wicked sorcerer Kastchey?"

Ivan stared at her blankly.

"It's not safe here," a soft voice broke in. It was the beautiful girl. "Kastchey hates visitors. If he finds you, he'll turn you to stone like the others." She pointed to a statue. "Please... go!"

"And what about you?" Ivan asked her. "Why are you here?"

"Kastchey captured the princess when we were walking with her," one of the other girls explained. "Now he holds her prisoner and we shall not leave her."

"Then neither will I," declared Ivan, gripping his dagger.

"It's no use," said the beautiful princess. "He can't be defeated. Save yourself." A mournful bell tolled six times as she was speaking. "We must go," she cried.

Lifting their skirts, the girls ran through the gates. Ivan dashed after them but he was too late. The gates, covered in twisted, lethal spikes, stayed firmly shut. As Ivan shook them frantically, there was a crash of thunder and lightning lit the sky.

The gates burned red-hot and Ivan jumped back, blowing on his blistering fingers. With a second crash, the gates burst open and a crowd of demons swarmed out. They had mean, pointed faces and vicious horns. One smiled cruelly, revealing sharp, dirty teeth. Their gnarled hands with gruesome talons reached for Ivan, clawing the air in front of him.

Ivan ran, darting among the statues, but there was no escape. The demons snatched at him and held on hard. Ivan fought back but the demons, who each had the strength of ten men, just held him tighter. Finally exhausted, Ivan slumped to the ground and a long shadow fell over him.

He looked up to see a fierce man glaring back. The man's face was lined with wrinkles, the skin hanging in folds around his fleshy nose. His thin lips were pressed together and his eyes were as black as night. A cloak, so old it was more green than black, flared around him and sparks flew out. "Kastchey!" thought Ivan.

The sorcerer brought his face close to Ivan's. "Trespasser!" he spat. "Since you like my garden so much, you shall stay in it!" Kastchey started to chant and Ivan shivered as an icy wind sprang up. A tingling began in his toes, followed by a cold, leaden feeling that spread over his feet and crept up his legs. Panicked, Ivan tried to move. He was stuck fast. Just then, a shower of golden sparks flew from Kastchey's cloak and Ivan remembered the Firebird's promise. By now, the chill had reached his arms, but with an effort he pulled out her feather.

In an instant, she was there, beating Kastchey back with her powerful wings. As she soared over the garden, the demons and Kastchey were entranced – forced to follow her in a jerky dance.

"Stop her!" the demons howled, but Kastchey was powerless. She kept them dancing until, with great sobs of pain, they collapsed. At last, Kastchey himself dropped to his knees.

Ivan raised his dagger, ready to plunge the glittering blade deep into the sorcerer's wicked heart.

"That... won't... kill... me," Kastchey sneered, gasping for breath.

The Firebird nodded. "It's true. He keeps his soul outside his body. It's in the blackened tree stump at the far corner of the garden. Go quickly Ivan," she begged. "I can't hold him for long."

Ivan raced down the garden, to return moments later with a large egg that gleamed like a pearl. "For something so evil, it looks beautiful," Ivan observed. He raised it above his head and the egg turned rosy pink in the setting sun.

"No!" Kastchey screamed, as Ivan brought the egg crashing down. Its shell smashed into a million pieces and thick green slime oozed out. At the same time, a cloud of evil-smelling smoke billowed up, and everything went black...

Scene Two

Kastchey and his demons were gone. So, a few days later, when the gates swung open again, it was to let out a crowd of gaily-dressed wedding guests. Ivan and the beautiful princess had fallen in love and were getting married. Music filled the garden as the princess's friends danced with men who only recently had been statues. As the happy couples spun around, fireworks exploded overhead – but the brightest light of all came from the Firebird.

Coppélia

Act One

Once upon a time, in a faraway village, there lived an old inventor named Dr. Coppélius. He had one daughter, Coppélia, and she was the talk of the village. Every day she sat on her balcony, quietly reading a book, but no one had ever heard her speak, or seen her move. Swanilda, one of the prettiest girls in the village, was fascinated by her.

"Perhaps today I'll see her move!" she thought, as she skipped into the village square. As she rounded the corner, Swanilda stopped in shock. There, in the middle of the square, was her boyfriend, Franz, blowing kisses up to Coppélia, with a look of adoration on his face.

"What are you doing, Franz?" cried Swanilda.

Franz spun around in surprise. He'd thought he was alone. "I... I..." he stammered.

"You flirt!" Swanilda said sharply. "She's not even interested in *you*."

Before Franz could answer, their friends swept into the square, skipping and whirling with excitement. Franz immediately joined in their dance, ignoring Swanilda.

"Oh Swanilda, have you heard?" said her best friend, breathlessly.

"Heard what?" asked Swanilda, trying to sound enthusiastic.

"The new village bell is going to ring for the first time tomorrow. We're all invited to the lord and lady's manor house. And guess what the bell will ring for?"

Swanilda stayed silent.

"It's going to ring for the new brides!" her friend nudged her and looked at Franz knowingly. "I'm sure you'll be one of them. Everyone thinks Franz will ask you to marry him."

Swanilda tried to answer, but she could only think of Franz blowing kisses to Coppélia, and her eyes filled with tears. Bowing her head, she dashed away from her friends.

By evening, the village square was quiet and empty. Only Dr. Coppélius was outside, stretching his old legs in the cool night air. He hummed to himself as he walked, lost in dreams about his latest invention. Then, to his horror, something leaped out at him from the darkness. Dr. Coppélius screamed and began to run, but seconds later he heard stifled giggles behind him. Spinning around, he saw a group of schoolboys shaking with laughter.

Dr. Coppélius was furious. "How dare you!" he shouted at the schoolboys. "Where's your respect? In my day we'd never dream of treating our elders like that." He waved around his walking stick, trying to whack the schoolboys on the legs, but they only laughed more and stuck out their tongues at him.

"Humph!" snorted Dr. Coppélius, as the last schoolboy finally disappeared from view. He went back into his house and slammed the door.

Swanilda and her friends rushed into the square. "What was all that noise about?" they asked each other. There was no one to be seen. After a quick glance around the square, the girls decided to go home. Swanilda lingered a while longer. She had spotted something bright and shiny on the dusty cobblestones and bent down to inspect it. "Wait!" she called after her friends, her voice brimming with excitement. "Look what I've found!"

"What is it?" asked her friends, rushing back to Swanilda.

Swanilda skipped with pleasure. "It's the key to Dr. Coppélius' house," she replied. "We can finally find out what he does all day."

"No way," said her friends, shaking their heads. "We're not going in there. No one's ever been inside Dr. Coppélius' house. It's not safe. And what about that strange girl, Coppélia?"

"She's probably fast asleep in bed," said Swanilda. "If you're not coming, then I'll go by myself." With these brave words she headed for the doctor's front door. Her friends looked at each other, guiltily.

"Wait, Swanilda," they called after her. "We're coming with you." The girls linked hands and, as quietly as they could, tiptoed into Dr. Coppélius' house.

Moments later, Franz crept into the square, carrying a ladder. He had his own plans to see Coppélia...

Act Two

The girls looked around Dr. Coppélius' workshop in terror. Figures hung by string from the ceiling and stared at them out of glassy eyes. Bodies stood stiff as stone against the walls, while others were slumped forward, or lay in a crumpled heap on the floor. It was deadly quiet.

"What is this place?" cried Swanilda's friends. "It's creepy."

"I don't know," Swanilda replied, in an awed whisper. She turned around and pulled back a curtain, coughing as clouds of dust filled the air. Then she gasped in surprise. Behind the curtain sat Coppélia, propped up in a chair.

"Hello," Swanilda said, as politely as she could.

There was no reply.

"What is it?" Swanilda asked. "Why won't you talk to me?"

But still Coppélia wouldn't answer.

"Fine!" snapped Swanilda finally. "Don't speak to me then," and she tugged angrily at Coppélia's skirt. But Coppélia sat as still as ever.

"I don't believe it…" began Swanilda. Inching even closer she peered right into Coppélia's face, then let out a giggle. "I know why Coppélia won't speak to us," she told her friends. "She's a doll!" Swanilda swept her arms around the room. "They're all dolls," she cried.

Forgetting to be quiet, the girls tore around the workshop, inspecting every doll they could find.

"Look!" said Swanilda. "Each doll has a key. Let's see what happens when we turn them."

As the girls wound the keys, the dolls sprang to life. A Scottish doll danced a jig, while a clown twirled around and around. Others played music – a jester bounced a bow across a violin, a pig plucked at a banjo and a small drummer boy went thump, thump, thump on his drum. Soon the workshop was full of jangling mechanical music and strange jerky dances. Swanilda and the girls whooped and danced along with delight.

Before long, Dr. Coppélius heard the noise. He burst into the room, shouting at the top of his voice, but the girls couldn't hear him above the music. "What do you think you're doing?" he cried, swinging his cane at their legs until they turned to look at him. "Get out of my workshop!"

The girls darted, and ran this way and that, leaping over his cane and out of the door.

Swanilda looked around in panic. She was trapped at the back of the workshop. "I'll never make it past Dr. Coppélius," she thought, and dived behind Coppélia's curtain. Swanilda sat as still as she could, holding her breath.

"My poor dolls," muttered Dr. Coppélius, thinking he was alone. He carefully put each doll back in its place, tenderly checking to see if they'd been scratched or torn. At that very moment, Franz entered the workshop. He clambered through the window and began sneaking around the room, looking for Coppélia. Dr. Coppélius couldn't believe it when he saw him.

"Another guest?" he drawled sarcastically. "And what have you come for, young man?"

Franz gasped with shock. "I've come to marry your daughter," he blurted out.

"Oh really?" said Dr. Coppélius, and a sinister smile spread across his face. "I'm very pleased to see you. Do sit down." He grabbed the dazed Franz by the arm and pulled him into a chair. "And what is your name?" he asked.

"F-F-F-Franz, sir," he stammered.

"Will you have some wine, Franz?" Dr. Coppélius went on smoothly. Without waiting for an answer, he turned his back on Franz and filled a glass. Then he quickly mixed in a powerful magic potion. He was almost shaking with excitement as he handed the drink to Franz.

"Thank you," Franz said as he took it, nervously gulping it down. Only later did Franz think the wine had a strange taste and then it was too late. The magic potion had started to take hold of him. His last memory was of the workshop swimming dizzily before his eyes, and then he was fast asleep.

Act Three

Dr. Coppélius rubbed his hands with glee. He carried Coppélia out from behind the curtain and placed her in the middle of his room. Then he consulted a magic book. "At last," he said to himself, "I can bring Coppélia to life."

He placed his hands first over Franz's eyes, then his arms and legs, to draw out his energy. Spinning around, Dr. Coppélius thrust the energy at Coppélia. For a moment nothing happened... until to Dr. Coppélius' joy, her eyes began to blink. Slowly, she rose from the chair and took a few stiff steps forward.

"I don't believe it!" cried Dr. Coppélius. "I'm a genius!" he laughed. "Now for the last step..." Focusing all his powers and muttering an ancient spell beneath his breath, he dragged his hand first across Franz's chest, and then across Coppélia's. A smile formed on Coppélia's lips and she began to breathe. "She's alive," shouted Dr. Coppélius. "My daughter's alive."

But Dr. Coppélius had been tricked. It wasn't Coppélia who began to dance around the room – it was Swanilda dressed in his daughter's clothes. The faster Swanilda danced, the more Dr. Coppélius jumped for joy. It was as if she knew every dance in the world. Dr. Coppélius threw her a tartan sash and Swanilda performed a Scottish jig. He handed her a fan, and – to his whoops and claps – she began a Spanish fandango.

As she twirled around the room, Swanilda caught sight of Franz, snoring in the chair. "I have to get us out of here," she thought. Each time she passed Franz, Swanilda tried to shake him awake. Franz slept on. "I know," thought Swanilda at last, "I'll distract Dr. Coppélius." She started to turn the keys of all the dolls, setting them in motion. Her dance gained in speed. She pushed with her hands and kicked with her legs, causing chaos wherever she went.

Dr. Coppélius stumbled after her. "Please, Coppélia," he begged, "do behave." As he bent to tend to his dolls, Swanilda quickly grabbed the sleeping Franz and dragged him out through the door.

When Dr. Coppélius turned around, Franz had gone. He looked for Coppélia, but all he saw was a twisted body on the floor. "Coppélia," he cried, bending down to pick her up. But her limbs fell lifeless from his grasp. "Did I dream it?" wondered Dr. Coppélius. "Did my daughter ever come to life at all?"

Act Four

Next morning, the sun shone brightly in the summer sky. All the villagers were gathered in the garden of the manor house. Birds sang from the trees, roses nodded their heads in the gentle breeze and the villagers chatted excitedly. The lord and lady of the manor had invited them all specially, for today marked the arrival of the new village bell.

"Welcome!" the lord declared. "We are not only celebrating the arrival of the bell. We will also be granting a blessing to all new brides and grooms – and giving each young couple a bag full of gold!"

A loud cheer went up from the crowd and they turned to see the brides and grooms dancing down the lawn. Franz and Swanilda led the parade. They leaped and twirled down the garden paths and skipped around trellises of flowers. Each groom lifted his bride high in the air, in celebration of his wedding day.

But a shadow fell across the lawn as Dr. Coppélius stumbled into the happy throng. In his arms he carried the broken Coppélia, wrapped in a blanket, her head lolling on his shoulders.

"I demand an explanation," he shouted. "My doll has been ruined and it will cost more than I own to mend her."

Swanilda and Franz stepped forward to meet him. "I'm sorry," said Swanilda. "We never meant to hurt you with our tricks. Here, take our bag of gold to mend Coppélia."

"I owe you more than gold," Franz added. "It was Coppélia who made me realize how much I love Swanilda – so much more than any other girl."

"Humph!" said Dr. Coppélius gruffly. He took their bag of gold and stomped away across the lawn, wanting to get back to his workshop, and his dolls, as quickly as possible.

Franz turned to Swanilda and wrapped her in his arms. "No more dolls for me," he said. "I give you my heart Swanilda."

"And I accept it," she replied. "Come on, let's join in the celebrations!"

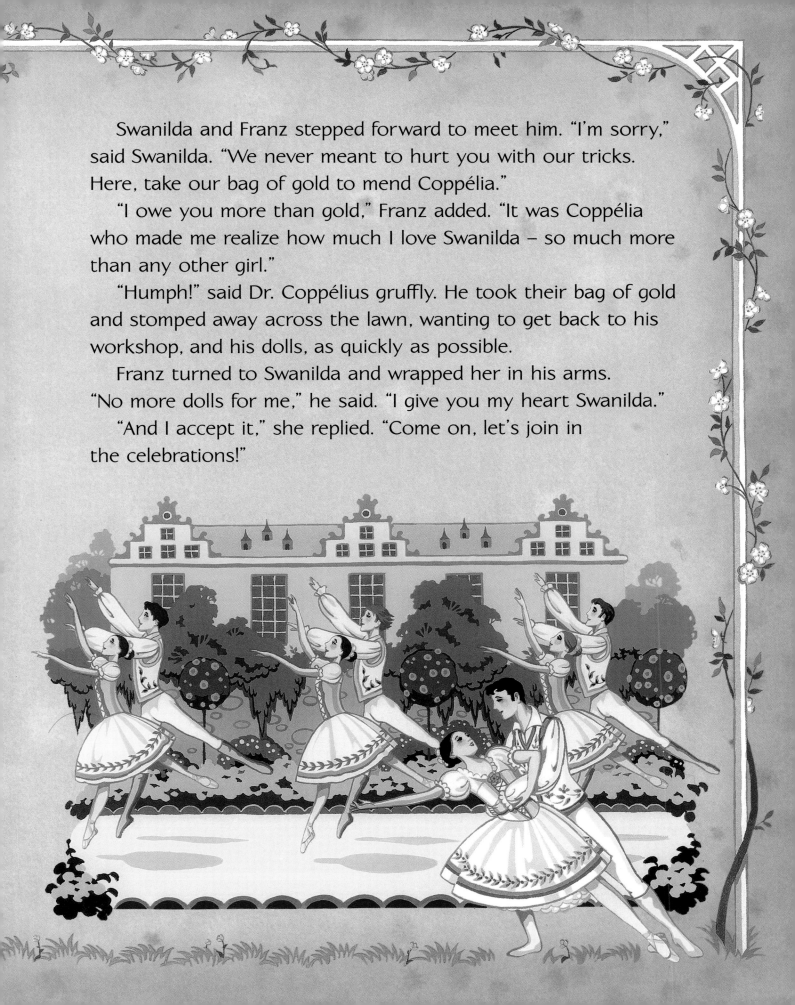

Cinderella

Act One

A large, run-down town house was basking in the late summer sun. Once, laughter and singing would have floated through its rooms but now the voices of two bossy sisters blasted from the windows. Today, they were arguing over an embroidered shawl.

"I'm wearing it to the ball," shouted the younger, shorter sister.

"No, I am!" yelled the older, taller one.

They both yanked at the shawl, pulling it this way and that, until it ripped in half. As they squabbled over whose fault it was, their beautiful stepsister, Cinderella, sat mending in the kitchen. She didn't own a pretty dress, let alone a silky shawl. And, though everyone was invited to the prince's ball that evening, Cinderella's horrible sisters wouldn't let her leave the house.

"I'd give anything to see the royal palace," she thought. Then she looked glumly across at the pile of dirty dishes. Her eyes settled on the little portrait of her mother on the mantelpiece. "Oh mother, if only you were still alive..."

Her thoughts were interrupted by footsteps and a gentle hand on her shoulder. "I thought I'd find you here," said Cinderella's father. He loved his daughter dearly, but he was never brave enough to stand up against her ghastly stepsisters. Picking up the portrait of his dead wife, his eyes filled with tears. "Life used to be so jolly," he said wistfully.

Just then, the two ugly sisters burst in.

"Lazing about as usual, Cinderella?" shrieked one.

"Leaving your poor sisters to dress for the ball on their own?" added the other.

"She's darning your socks," said Cinderella's father, timidly.

"Don't give her excuses," the tall sister snapped. "Now Cinderella, my dainty toenails need trimming."

"And my nose hairs need plucking," added the other.

Cinderella was saved from these gruesome tasks by a jangle on the door bell. An old beggarwoman stood hunched on the steps. "Could you spare me a crumb to eat?" she croaked. Dashing back to the kitchen, Cinderella found the bread roll she'd saved for her supper and handed it to the old woman.

"Don't give her anything!" cried the elder sister, stomping between them. She was about to say more but a wave of the beggarwoman's stick stuck her lips together.

Then, in a flash, the beggarwoman disappeared.

Ding-a-ling. Immediately, the doorbell rang again. It was the dressmaker with outfits for the ugly sisters. *Ding-a-ling.* The shoemaker entered with their pointy shoes. *Ding-a-ling.* Two feathered hats arrived in big boxes. *Ding-a-ling.* A hairdresser entered and bowed. Overcome with excitement, the ugly sisters struggled to get ready. They squeezed themselves into corsets, streaked their faces with lipstick and eyeliner, and pinned elaborate wigs to their hair.

Ding-a-ling. This time it was the dance teacher.

"Copy me," he said, taking graceful steps forward.

The ugly sisters stumbled flat-footed across the room.

"Try again," he said calmly. This time the short sister tripped over her dress. He took her hand to steady her, but that made the tall sister jealous. Finally, the teacher gave up and politely excused himself. It was time for the ball.

"Don't we look divine," cooed the sisters.

Cinderella thought it best not to answer. She led her father to the door and the ugly sisters whisked him away.

"Peace and quiet at last," thought Cinderella. Then, with a giggle, she picked up her broom and began to dance. Round and round she twirled, her dainty feet hardly touching the ground, until a flourish of music made her look up. There stood the beggarwoman.

"How... who... aren't you the woman I gave the bread to?" stammered Cinderella.

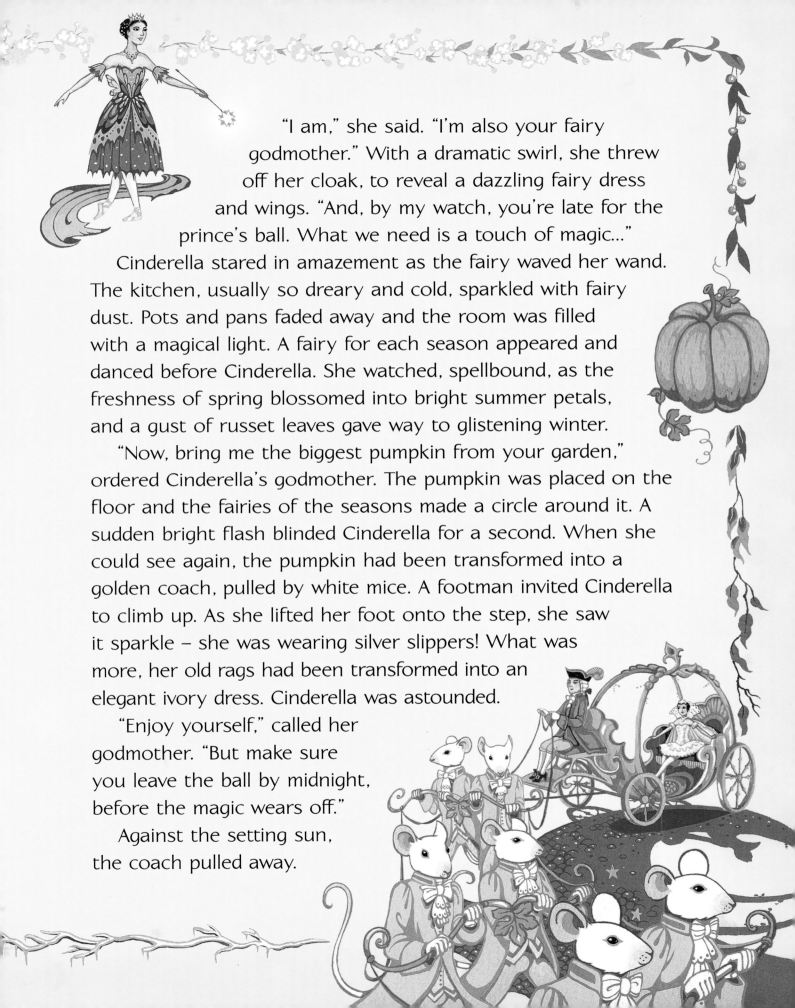

"I am," she said. "I'm also your fairy godmother." With a dramatic swirl, she threw off her cloak, to reveal a dazzling fairy dress and wings. "And, by my watch, you're late for the prince's ball. What we need is a touch of magic..."

Cinderella stared in amazement as the fairy waved her wand. The kitchen, usually so dreary and cold, sparkled with fairy dust. Pots and pans faded away and the room was filled with a magical light. A fairy for each season appeared and danced before Cinderella. She watched, spellbound, as the freshness of spring blossomed into bright summer petals, and a gust of russet leaves gave way to glistening winter.

"Now, bring me the biggest pumpkin from your garden," ordered Cinderella's godmother. The pumpkin was placed on the floor and the fairies of the seasons made a circle around it. A sudden bright flash blinded Cinderella for a second. When she could see again, the pumpkin had been transformed into a golden coach, pulled by white mice. A footman invited Cinderella to climb up. As she lifted her foot onto the step, she saw it sparkle – she was wearing silver slippers! What was more, her old rags had been transformed into an elegant ivory dress. Cinderella was astounded.

"Enjoy yourself," called her godmother. "But make sure you leave the ball by midnight, before the magic wears off."

Against the setting sun, the coach pulled away.

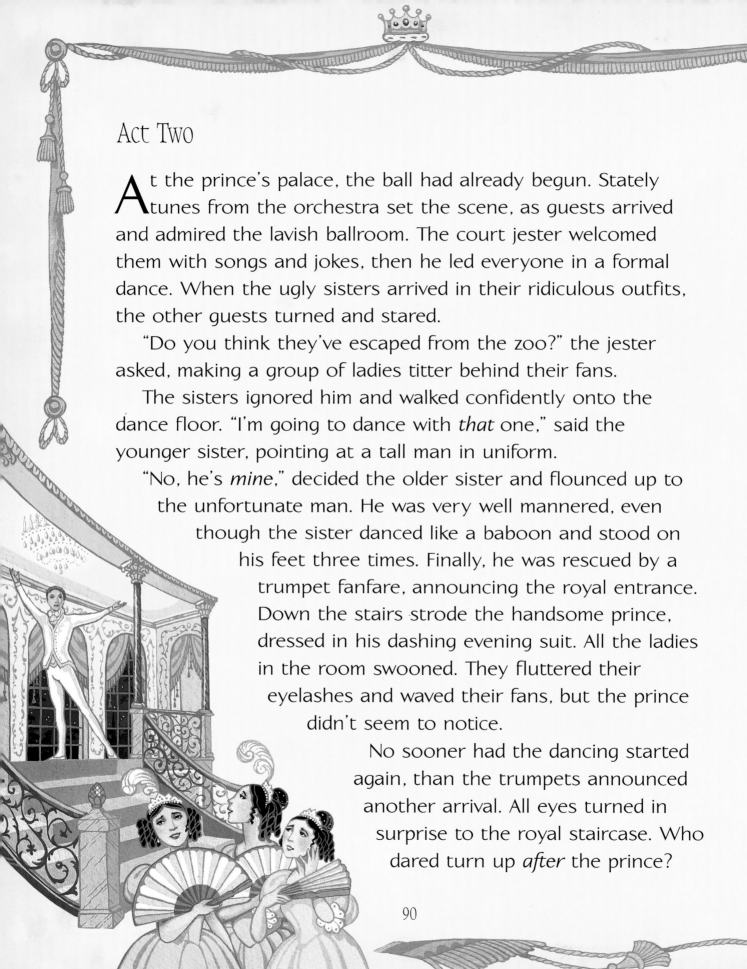

Act Two

At the prince's palace, the ball had already begun. Stately tunes from the orchestra set the scene, as guests arrived and admired the lavish ballroom. The court jester welcomed them with songs and jokes, then he led everyone in a formal dance. When the ugly sisters arrived in their ridiculous outfits, the other guests turned and stared.

"Do you think they've escaped from the zoo?" the jester asked, making a group of ladies titter behind their fans.

The sisters ignored him and walked confidently onto the dance floor. "I'm going to dance with *that* one," said the younger sister, pointing at a tall man in uniform.

"No, he's *mine*," decided the older sister and flounced up to the unfortunate man. He was very well mannered, even though the sister danced like a baboon and stood on his feet three times. Finally, he was rescued by a trumpet fanfare, announcing the royal entrance. Down the stairs strode the handsome prince, dressed in his dashing evening suit. All the ladies in the room swooned. They fluttered their eyelashes and waved their fans, but the prince didn't seem to notice.

No sooner had the dancing started again, than the trumpets announced another arrival. All eyes turned in surprise to the royal staircase. Who dared turn up *after* the prince?

90

Framed by the palace window, there stood Cinderella in her magical dress. At the sight of all the guests, she almost ran away. Then she took a deep breath and slowly descended the stairs. Everyone stared in wonder, including the prince. He offered Cinderella his hand and guided her onto the dance floor. Without saying a word, they began to dance, as if they had danced together all their lives.

"She's so graceful," whispered one of the guests.

"She must be a princess," added another.

On the edge of the dance floor, the ugly sisters were sulking. "Why won't he dance with me?" said the tall one.

"Because he prefers me," teased her sister.

When the dance came to an end, the prince called for oranges – the most exotic fruit in his kingdom. He presented one to Cinderella as a sign of his love. Taking pity on the ugly sisters, he gave them oranges too. While they bickered over whose was the biggest, the prince and Cinderella tiptoed away. Gazing grumpily across the ballroom, the sisters realized no one was going to ask them to dance. So, in the end, they linked arms and danced with each other.

Meanwhile, Cinderella and the prince were lost in a dream. They danced across the moonlit terrace, into the garden and back to the ballroom. Floating on happiness, they both wished the evening would last forever. But the hours whirled by and Cinderella heard her godmother's warning in her ear. Then came the chiming of the palace clock.

"It's midnight!" she cried in a panic.

"Don't worry," hushed the prince, holding her close.

"But I must go," she said sadly.

Cinderella had to slip under the prince's arm to escape. A wall of dancing guests stood between her and the door. She darted between them and fled the palace only just in time. Already her dress had turned back into rags.

The poor prince rushed after her, but in vain. All that was left of his enchanting princess was a dainty silver slipper.

Act Three

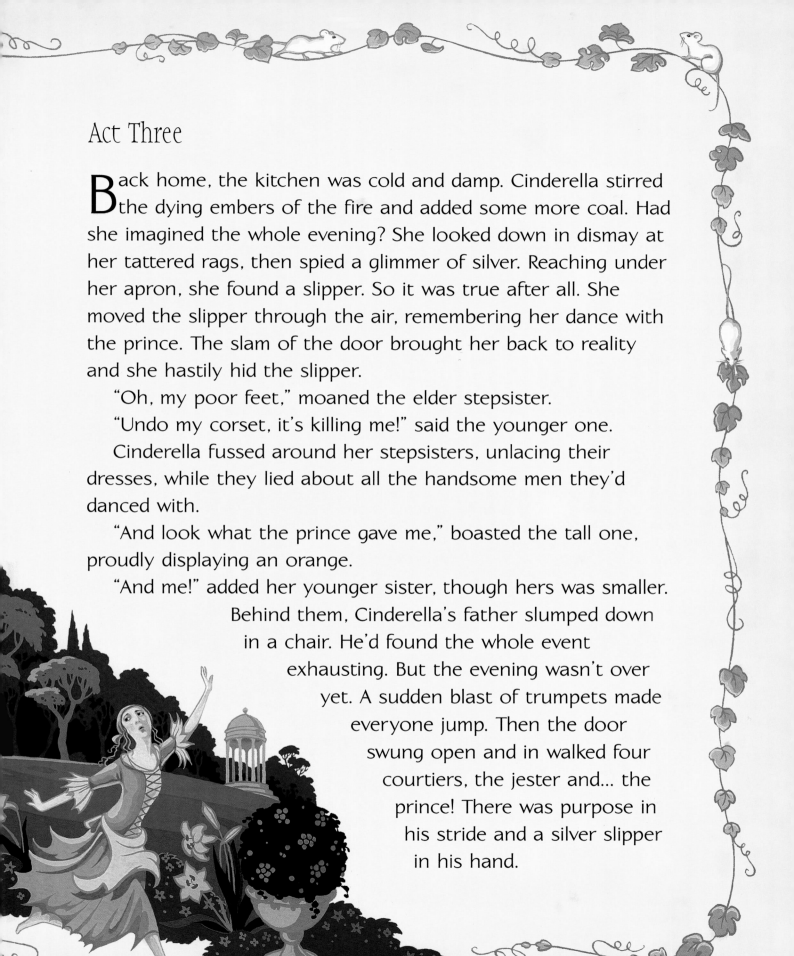

Back home, the kitchen was cold and damp. Cinderella stirred the dying embers of the fire and added some more coal. Had she imagined the whole evening? She looked down in dismay at her tattered rags, then spied a glimmer of silver. Reaching under her apron, she found a slipper. So it was true after all. She moved the slipper through the air, remembering her dance with the prince. The slam of the door brought her back to reality and she hastily hid the slipper.

"Oh, my poor feet," moaned the elder stepsister.

"Undo my corset, it's killing me!" said the younger one.

Cinderella fussed around her stepsisters, unlacing their dresses, while they lied about all the handsome men they'd danced with.

"And look what the prince gave me," boasted the tall one, proudly displaying an orange.

"And me!" added her younger sister, though hers was smaller. Behind them, Cinderella's father slumped down in a chair. He'd found the whole event exhausting. But the evening wasn't over yet. A sudden blast of trumpets made everyone jump. Then the door swung open and in walked four courtiers, the jester and... the prince! There was purpose in his stride and a silver slipper in his hand.

"I intend to marry the girl whose foot fits this slipper," he announced, "and I'll travel the kingdom until I find her."

"Travel no further," cried the tall sister, wrenching off her stiletto. "It's me!" She snatched the slipper from him and tried to ram it onto her foot. The slipper barely covered her toes.

"Let me try!" cried her sister. "It's definitely my size." But no amount of squeezing and tugging could make the slipper fit.

"Are there any more girls in this house?" asked the prince.

Before Cinderella's father could speak, the ugly sisters shouted, "Of course not! Only us."

Cinderella crept into the shadows, praying the prince wouldn't see her. She wanted him to remember her as a stunning princess, not a scullery maid. But as she moved, the slipper fell from her pocket. It twinkled in the fire glow and caught the prince's eye. He rushed forward and held his slipper to it. They matched! Looking up in excitement, he saw Cinderella.

"Please try on this slipper," he asked her gently.

The jester brought forward a chair and everyone else gathered around to watch. Timidly, Cinderella sat down, not daring to look the prince in the eye. Kneeling by her side, he easily fitted the slipper on her slender foot.

"The princess from the ball!" he cried, taking her in his arms.

"No, I'm only a poor girl in rags," said Cinderella with a sigh.

"Then marry me and become my princess!"

Cinderella looked up at the prince and they started to dance as they'd done at the ball.

The stepsisters were horrified. Now the girl they'd always bullied would one day be queen. Curtseying and cooing, they begged for her forgiveness.

"Of course I forgive you," said the starry-eyed Cinderella.

As she spoke, a magical glow filled the room. The fairy godmother glided in, her smile reaching from cheek to cheek. With a flurry of wings, the other fairies appeared behind her. The setting swiftly changed and Cinderella found herself in the palace gardens once more. This time, she would never have to leave her prince.

Acknowledgements

The publishers are grateful to the following for permission to reproduce material:

pages 6-7 © Paul Barton/CORBIS; **pages 20-21** © Ann Johansson/CORBIS;
pages 28-29 The Royal Ballet, Jonathan Cope and Darcey Bussell, The Nutcracker, Angela Taylor;
page 30 (top and middle) © V&A Images/Theatre Museum, (bottom) © Hulton-Deutsch
Collection/CORBIS; **page 31** (top) © Topham Picturepoint/ArenaPAL, (bottom) © Lebrecht Music Collection/Alamy;
page 32 (top) © Bettman/CORBIS, bottom © Hulton-Deutsch Collection/CORBIS;
page 33 (top) © ArenaPAL, (bottom) © Leslie E. Spatt; **page 34** (left) © Eric Richmond/ArenaPAL;
(bottom) © The Royal Ballet, Darcey Bussell and Jonathan Cope, Tryst, Bill Cooper;
page 35 Carlos Acosta quotation www.ballet.co.uk, (top) © Clive Barda/ArenaPAL,
(bottom) © The Royal Ballet, Alina Cojocaru and Johan Kobborg, Bill Cooper;
pages 36-37 © The Royal Ballet, The Nutcracker, Angela Taylor

Every effort has been made to trace and acknowledge ownership of copyright. If any rights have been omitted,
the publishers offer to rectify this in any subsequent editions following notification.